IT'S TRUE!
PIRATES
ATE RATS

Did you know that frogs are cannibals,
fashion can be fatal and the dinosaurs
never died? Or that redheads were
once burned at the stake as witches?
Find out why rubbish tips are like lasagna,
and how maggots help solve crimes!

Heather Catchpole
& Vanessa Woods
PICTURES BY Mic Looby

IT'S TRUE!

PIRATES

ATE RATS

ALLEN&UNWIN

First published in 2007

Allen & Unwin
83 Alexander Street
Crows Nest NSW 2065
Australia
Phone: (61 2) 8425 0100
Fax: (61 2) 9906 2218
Email: info@allenandunwin.com
Web: www.allenandunwin.com

National Library of Australia
Cataloguing-in-Publication entry:

Catchpole, Heather.
It's true! pirates ate rats.
Bibliography.
Includes index.
For primary aged children.
ISBN 978 1 74114 607 3.
1. Pirates – Juvenile literature. I. Woods, Vanessa.
II. Title. (Series : It's true! ; 27)
910.45

Series, cover and text design by Ruth Grüner
Cover photograph: Jason van der Valk/istockphoto.com (background),
Photodisc/Getty Images (pirate), Dave King/Dorling Kindersley
collection/Getty Images (rat), Emilia Stasiak/istockphoto.com (rodents)
Set in 12.5pt Minion by Ruth Grüner
Printed by McPherson's Printing Group

1 3 5 7 9 10 8 6 4 2

**Teaching notes for the It's True! series are available
on the website: www.itstrue.com.au**

CONTENTS

Why pirates?

For thousands of years they've raided the seas, kidnapped innocent people, and struck terror into the hearts of sailors. Through the centuries their clothes and names have changed but one thing hasn't – the fascination these daring criminals hold for us. Tales of pirates have been told and retold so many times that it's hard to separate truth from fiction. But we do know one thing for sure – pirates were bloodthirsty murderers, thieves and outlaws.

Do you think you could be a pirate? Read this book to find out how and why people turn to piracy. Discover what life was really like on board a pirate ship. Could you kill someone for a bag of gold? Would you risk death every day to chase dreams on the open sea? And finally, if you really had to . . . would you eat rats?

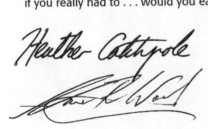

1

ROBBERS, ROVERS AND RASCALS

There's a story that over 2000 years ago, pirates captured the famous Roman emperor Julius Caesar. Caesar asked how much he was being ransomed for.

'Twenty talents,' the pirates replied (meaning 'Heaps' – twenty talents would be worth almost $500 000 today).

'Is that all?' cried Julius Caesar. 'I'm worth much more than that – double it!'

Caesar was held captive for 38 days. He spent his

time joining in the pirates' games and yelling at them if they made too much noise when he was trying to sleep. He even read them his poetry, calling anyone who didn't like his work 'illiterate barbarians' (brutes who couldn't read).

The pirates grew fond of Caesar, who was only a young man at the time, but that didn't mean Caesar let them off the hook. He told the pirates that once he was free again he would crucify the lot of them. Sure enough, as soon as he was released, he kept his promise.

Tales of revenge

There were pirate stories before Julius Caesar. A Greek myth tells of pirates who kidnapped Dionysus, the god of wine. They demanded a ransom, but Dionysus changed himself into a lion and the terrified pirates jumped overboard. In revenge, Dionysus turned them into dolphins that chased ships ever after. They still do today.

Another legend tells of the famous leader of the ancient Macedonians, Alexander the Great. Alexander captured a notorious pirate and gave him a chance to beg for forgiveness before he was executed.

'Why should I?' the pirate replied. 'You and I are the same, except I only steal from a few people while you plunder whole countries at a time.'

The truth about pirates

So just what are pirates? Do you think of them as daredevil adventurers with earrings, swords and cutlasses? Or as outlaws who made anyone that defied them walk the plank?

Ideas like this come from the hundreds of books, plays and movies written about pirates, rather than facts.

In reality, pirates came from all walks of life. They wore whatever clothes they could get their hands on, and often went hungry. Walking the plank was made famous by the

fictional pirate Captain Hook in
Peter Pan, but there are almost
no records of real-life pirates
making prisoners walk the
plank. It was much less
trouble for pirates to
pitch their prisoners
over the side, or run
them through with
a sword.

Anyone who
robs for profit, on the
sea or along the shore,
is a pirate. Ever since
people invented boats and
started sending gold, gems, cloth or even food across
the ocean, pirates have been trying to rob them.

There were probably pirates way back in history –
in ancient Egypt and Mesopotamia (where the earliest
boats were built around 2500 BC) and Phoenicia.
Later, pirates preyed on the wealthy shipping of the
Mycenaeans, Greeks and Romans.

In the 800s and 900s, Europe was at the mercy of Danish pirates and Vikings who roamed the cold northern seas in longboats powered with rows of oars. They attacked coastal villages and took slaves to row their boats. From the 1100s on, Chinese junks that could enter shallow waters were employed by pirates to pillage villages along the south Chinese coast. In the early 1600s, the infamous Barbary Coast corsairs (another word for pirates) terrorised the Mediterranean.

The word 'pirate' comes from the Latin *pirata*, which in turn comes from the Greek word *peirates* or *peirao*, meaning attempt or assault.

Pirate lingo

Here are some of the words you might meet in this book.

Black spot: To put the black spot on a pirate
is to sentence him to death

Davy Jones' locker: The bottom of the ocean,
signifying death

Deadlights: A heavy shutter for a window or porthole, also
slang for eyes

Gangway: A passageway on a ship, or a signal
to get out of the way!

Go on the account: Start the pirate adventure
and go after some booty!

Heave to: To turn a ship so that its bow (front) heads into
the wind and the ship lies drifting

Jack Ketch: Hangman

Landlubber: Someone who has no experience at sea

Lights: Lungs

Poxy: Diseased

Sail ho: I see a ship

Strike the colours: Bring down the flag
and surrender

Swab: A mop used to clean the deck, but also
an insult meaning a stupid person

Treasure fleet of the Americas

The most famous era of pirates, when pirates like Blackbeard and Captain Kidd sailed the seas, began with the discovery of America.

In 1519, the Spanish conquistadors (meaning 'conquerers') followed Christopher Columbus to explore America, the New World. They journeyed deep into the heart of the jungle, following rumours of *ciudades d'oro* – cities of gold. What they found was beyond their wildest imagination. They stumbled upon temples lined with gold and silver that sparkled in the sunlight.

The Incas, who called themselves the children of the Sun, built these temples. They believed gold was the sweat of the sun and silver was the tears of the moon. Gold and silver had no commercial value to the Incas, but they loved them for their beauty and used them for craft ornaments, or to adorn temples and grand houses.

The metals that held no value to the Incas became their downfall. The Spanish plundered the temples and killed anyone who stood in their way. Those who were left alive were sold as slaves, or put to work in mines, digging for more precious jewels and metals.

Spain set up colonies throughout the Americas that produced silver, gold, emeralds, pearls, silks, indigo (a blue dye) and spices. In just four years between 1596 and 1600, the Spanish made 34 438 500 pesos, about $1 billion in today's money.

To keep control over their colonies, Spain passed a law that forbade the colonies to trade with any except Spanish ships. Twice a year Spanish fleets sailed down the coast of America delivering supplies to the colonies and returned loaded with riches for Spain. The ships, which became known as the Treasure Fleet, kept sailing for over 300 years.

A French captain, Jean Fleury, captured three of the Spanish treasure ships in 1523. News of the 200 kilograms of gold dust and 400 kilograms of pearls, emeralds and other gems Fleury had stolen reached the ears of the French king, Francis I. He demanded other captains become privateers – pirates who worked for governments – to capture more of this wonderful wealth. England also sent privateers to the Caribbean and South America, and other pirates began to prey on the ships as they crossed the Atlantic.

The Golden Age of pirates had begun.

A plague of pirates on you all!

Between about 1650 and the early 1700s, pirates had great success, particularly in the Caribbean. With their light, fast ships they evaded capture, and when their ships got old or damaged, they simply stole another one. Often pirates had excellent local knowledge of the area, so if anyone came after them, they could vanish into hidden swamps, rivers and islands.

Piracy was a quick if risky way to get rich in the new colonies and towns of the West Indies. Often, governors of the towns turned a blind eye to piracy in return for a share of the loot. Some governors even hired pirates to attack the ships of other nations.

Places like Port Royal, St Anne and Tortuga became pirate towns, where pirates could land to trade and waste their wealth.

Never on Sunday

The Caribbean pirates had their own flags, and their own laws or code of behaviour. The laws were every bit as strict as your parents' rules at home. They helped keep the peace during long voyages and settled any disputes that broke out over the division of loot.

The pirates swore to keep the code, promising to uphold it in the same way that people in court swear over the Bible – although instead of a Bible pirates may have sworn on a flag, or a cutlass.

Different captains had different codes. The code of the ferocious female pirate Ching Shih stated that any food or provisions taken from poor coastal villages must be paid for. Any crew member who didn't stick to the code could be sliced with a knife down the nose or the ears.

Captain Bartholomew Roberts (Black Bart) banned any form of gambling on his ship and decreed a day of rest on Sundays, even for the ship's musicians. He also ordered the lights on board to be put out at 8 p.m. every night!

Roberts' rules

Here's a shortened version of Bartholomew Roberts' code.

(i) Every man shall have an equal vote in important decisions. Everyone will have an equal share of any food or liquor seized from another ship.

(ii) Every man shall be called fairly in turn because over and above their proper share, they are allowed a shift of clothes. Anyone who takes more than his share of gold, silver, jewels or money to the value of even one dollar, will be marooned. If any man rob another he shall have his nose and ears slit, and be put ashore where he shall be sure to encounter hardships.

(iii) No one shall game [gamble] for money with either dice or cards.

(iv) Lights and candles should be put out at eight at night. If any of the crew wants to drink after that hour, they must sit upon the open deck without lights.

(v) Each man shall keep his piece [gun], cutlass and pistols at all times clean and ready for action.

(vi) No boy or woman is allowed among the crew. Any man found seducing a woman and carrying her to sea in disguise will suffer death.

(vii) Anyone who deserts the ship during a battle will be punished by death or marooning.

(viii) No striking another man on board. All quarrels will be ended on shore by a duel, using pistols. If both miss their aim, they fight with cutlasses. Whoever draws first blood is the victor.

(ix) No man shall talk of quitting piracy till each has a share of 1000 pounds. Every man who shall become a cripple or lose a limb in the service shall have 800 pieces of eight [silver coins]. Lesser injuries will get lesser payments.

(x) Treasure gained will be split such that the captain and the quartermaster shall each receive two shares, the master gunner and boatswain one and a half shares each, all other officers one and a quarter, and private gentlemen of fortune one share each.

(xi) The musicians have the right to rest on the Sabbath Day [Sunday]. On all other days they must perform unless by special favour of the Captain.

2

THE LIFE OF A PIRATE: HUNGRY AND HUNTED

A pirate's life was dangerous. Pirates fought on land and sea to secure money, ships and prisoners. They fought merchants, navies, armies and often each other, risking death by sword or cannonball in a ferocious sea battle. Along the way you could be flogged by your captain, hunted by privateers, or prey to starvation on long sea voyages. Welcome on board, me hearties!

Despite the perils of battle, the biggest killer of
pirates was disease caused by a poor diet.

Rum, rats or cabbage

Dinner on a pirate ship might include an egg from
one of the chickens on board, if you were lucky.
Fortunate pirates of the Caribbean dined on turtles,
which they caught on desert (deserted) islands,
or on tuna and dolphins. But most of the time pirates
went hungry. They ate biscuits made from flour and
water that were often crawling
with so many weevils that
pirates ate them in the dark,
or tapped them against tables
to remove the weevils. Some
pirates were so hungry they ate their
leather bags, rats, and occasionally
their prisoners!

Pirates had almost no fresh fruit
and vegetables, and therefore no
vitamin C in their diet. Why does

that matter? Well, people who lack this vitamin soon develop the symptoms of scurvy. It starts with spots on the skin and bleeding gums. Then they become depressed and tired, and before too long they die.

Captain Cook was one of the first to introduce cabbages to his ships' menus, to prevent scurvy. (He could have used oranges or any of several other fruits and vegetables.) But many pirate captains were far more likely to fill up the stores with rum than cabbages!

Cramped conditions below deck meant that pirates could easily catch all sorts of diseases from each other. Captain William Kidd, a Scottish pirate who roamed from Africa to America in the late

1600s, lost a third of his crew to cholera. This bacterial disease can be cured today by antibiotics, which weren't discovered until the 1940s.

Disease wasn't the only threat to Kidd's crew. William Kidd was famed for his cruelty (see chapter 6) and once strung a man to the mast and clubbed him with a cutlass. He was also tried for murder after killing one of his crew with an iron bucket. In a pirate's world, torture, cruelty and punishment were part of daily life.

Fleeing from justice

Soldiers, privateers (government-sponsored pirates) and anyone after prize money hunted pirates. British naval ships would sometimes force pirate crews into the Royal Navy, where the work was often harsher and more demanding, with little chance of reward.

In between battles and money-wasting spells on land were long periods at sea. In the 1600s ships could sail for months on end with no land in sight. Water quickly became polluted on board, so pirates drank rum, beer or wine. Drunk, bored and hungry, they often became quarrelsome or dissatisfied. They might even plan to mutiny, ganging up on the captain to force him to do what they wanted. When Captain Kidd heard that first mate Robert Culliford was leading a mutiny, he ordered his crew to attack. He was in for a nasty surprise. Most of the crew chose to join Culliford, leaving Kidd and his ship with a loyal crew of just 13 out of around 150.

Marooned!

Being marooned was one of the things that people feared most from pirates. Beware all ye who break the pirate code, you'll be left on a desert island with naught to eat but sand!

Scottish privateer Alexander Selkirk was marooned on an island for five whole years. His captain left him there in 1704, deciding he was too troublesome to keep on board. (Selkirk had tried to persuade some of the crew to abandon their leaky ship, the *Cinque Ports* – which indeed later sank.) When another privateer,

Captain Rogers, and his crew dropped anchor on the South Pacific islands of Juan Fernández five years later, they were greeted by Selkirk, dressed in goatskin and looking like a savage. He had survived by making fire with sticks, eating goats, and taming wild cats to stop the rats chewing on his feet at night. Selkirk was the inspiration for Daniel Defoe's famous novel *Robinson Crusoe*.

Not everyone was so lucky. Usually being stuck on a desert island meant a slow, horrible death. With no water, food or fire, most of the marooned pirates used their last bullet (left to them by right of pirate code) on themselves.

X marks the spot ~ or does it?

Leaving your crew marooned was one thing, but leaving your treasure was quite another. Tales of pirates often tell of fabulous treasure buried on little-known islands. In Robert Louis Stevenson's book, *Treasure Island*, Jim Hawkins goes in search of the buried treasure of the dreaded Captain Flint. In real life, few pirates would have buried their treasure. They spent most of their money on drinking and gambling while they were in port,

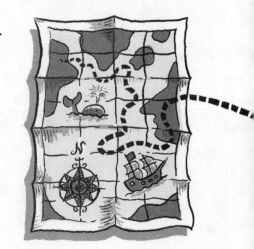

and never had money left over to save, much less bury.

In 1695 Henry Avery and his crew captured a treasure ship of the Mughal Emperor of India that carried cargo worth over half a billion dollars in today's money. Each man received the equivalent of over $3 million. Avery was so rich that he was able to retire and live the rest of his life in luxury. With such wealth, a pirate could give up the hazards of piracy and drink and be merry for evermore!

The greatest treasure hunt of all was for the ship of Sam Bellamy. Known as 'Black Sam', Bellamy captured the slave ship *Whydah* in 1717. With it he gained one of the richest hauls of gold, silver, ivory, indigo and sugar ever captured. But luck was against Black Sam and the *Whydah* was caught in a violent storm and swept towards the coast. Bellamy ordered his men to cut the anchors but the ship struck a reef and began to break apart. Bellamy drowned and only two men survived.

The remains of the ship were found in 1984. In it were 8357 silver coins, 17 gold bars and hundreds of pieces of African jewellery. The treasure was said to be worth over half a billion dollars.

If you're looking to find some buccaneer booty of your own – be warned. The wreck of the *Whydah* is the only pirate ship ever found that had any treasure on board.

Hauling up treasure from the seabed

Recovering the treasure from a sunken ship is rarely easy. The ship may be stuck in dangerous seas on a reef or in a strong current, or buried beneath shifting sands in hundreds of metres of seawater.

Bringing up sunken cargoes can involve some high-tech equipment, including sonar, underwater remote-controlled vehicles and magnetometers towed behind searching ships to locate metal objects in a wreck. A few spectacular recoveries have been made, such as the 600 barrels of gold and Incan jewels that were discovered in September 2005 on Robinson Crusoe Island near Chile. In 1715, Spanish general Juan Esteban Ubilla y Echeverria reportedly buried the treasure (possibly to keep it from pirates), and died in a shipwreck on his way back to Spain. Treasure hunters had been on the lookout for it ever since.

3

PIRATE GEAR – PISTOLS, BOOTS AND BANDANNAS

Pirates dressed much like the sailors and merchants of their time. The ones who cruised the Caribbean in the 1500s and 1600s wore baggy pants and knee-high stockings, thigh-length jackets belted with scarves, leather boots and broad-brimmed hats or bandannas on their heads. Naval uniforms weren't introduced until 1748 for British sailors.

Make-up please!

Some pirates were renowned for their fancy gear. The barbaric Bartholomew Roberts wore a crimson waistcoat and breeches, a feathered hat and heavy jewellery (stolen, of course).

Weapons of destruction

Pirates in movies and plays are often shown fighting with thin swords called rapiers. In reality, pirates of

Ear-piercing tales

Did sailors wear earrings? Yes, they did. As a kind of charm to protect themselves from the sea, sailors would buy two gold rings before setting sail. One would be cut and pressed into the shape of an earring and inserted into the sailor's ear. The other was cast into the sea as an offering to Davy Jones – the mythical death spirit of the deep. Men today still wear earrings in one of their ears – but probably don't throw the other one into the sea!

the 1600s used weapons similar to those used by other sailors – some pirates had been in the Navy and kept their naval weapons when they turned to piracy.

The weapons of a Caribbean pirate included flintlock pistols – guns filled with gunpowder and lit with a steel flint. These guns were very inaccurate. They also had to be cleaned constantly, particularly in the wet, salty conditions aboard ship. Pirates who didn't keep their weapons primed and cleaned risked severe punishment. Pirates also carried short daggers, like the dirk used in the English Navy, and boarding axes.

Pirate ships sometimes carried brass and bronze cannons, but usually they tried to take their prey by surprise rather than by force. They would try to board the other ship in the night and for this they needed their hand weapons.

The pirates of the East terrorised the island peoples of the Indian Ocean and preyed on Indian and European shipping in the 1800s. They used similar weapons to those of the Caribbean pirates, but also carried spears and poison-tipped arrows that they shot through blowpipes.

Pirates were merciless in making people confess where they had hidden their treasure. When Dona Agustin de Rojas from Portobelo was captured by pirates in 1668, she stood naked in a barrel of gunpowder while a pirate threatened to drop in a lighted taper unless she told him where she had hidden

27

her gold. Other victims were whipped, burned and horribly tortured by pirates who wanted their riches.

Another reason pirates tortured people was to terrify everyone into surrendering as soon as they saw a pirate ship. If pirates let everyone go unharmed, then no one would give up easily. Pirates didn't want to fight. They risked getting captured or killed.

For those unlucky enough to be chased by pirates, there was a general rule: surrender and you'll go free, fight and you'll all die. But this wasn't written into pirate codes, and some pirates tortured and killed their victims anyway.

Hoist the Union Jack, me hearties

In the golden age of pirates, ships had no radios. Instead, ships flew a flag high on their mast so anyone approaching would know what country they were from.

Pirates wanted to get right up close to a ship before they struck, so they often tried to disguise themselves.

They kept several flags on board. If the ship they were chasing flew an English flag, the pirates would hoist up a Union Jack as well. If the ship flew a French flag, the pirates would hoist up the same red, white and blue stripes. The sailors on the target ship would think they were friends, and might even slow down to catch up on any news. As the pirate ship approached, it unfurled a flag that struck terror into the heart of every sailor – the Jolly Roger.

Most people think of a pirate flag as being black with a white skull and crossbones. This flag was flown by some pirates, but there were other designs. Black Bartholomew Roberts had a flag showing a pirate with a drawn sword standing on the skulls of two men. Blackbeard had a skeleton devil with its sword aimed straight at a bleeding heart. All pirate flags were meant to cause fear and panic. They could be red or black, with a skull to symbolise death, an hourglass to symbolise limited time, or bleeding hearts. A plain red flag indicated the pirates would give no quarter (meaning they'd kill all on board) and was probably the most dreaded flag of all.

Occasionally, a ship would refuse to surrender, and then the pirates were prepared to uphold their flag and fight. Once within range they would fire their cannons. Cannons could fire scattered lead shot or cannonballs. They were often inaccurate, but 20 cannons all firing at once could shatter the whole side of a ship.

When the pirates were close enough, they threw grappling hooks onto the enemy ship, and used them to pull the two vessels together. Then, with fierce screams and yells to put terror into the heart of all, they would board the ship.

Pants, please!

What did pirates most want to steal? Some surprising things: other men's britches, and bandages and bottles of medicine for starters.

Everyday items such as clothing, food and water soon became scarce after a long voyage at sea, and yet buying new gear was dangerous when the law lay waiting at every port. It was easier to steal them. Unlucky sailors and merchants caught by pirates might lose their pants as well as their merchandise. Benjamin Hornigold once stole every hat on board a captured ship.

Navigational tools were vital for pirates. A compass gave the north, south, east or west bearing, and a sextant measured the angle of the sun or stars above the horizon. Sextants, and similar instruments called quadrants and octants, allowed an experienced navigator to find his latitude, the distance of the ship from the equator.

A pirate ship needed to set a course along the popular trading routes of the day, as this was the most likely place to find a prize ship. Being able to find the nearest safe port or island hideaway was also crucial. Captains who got lost faced mutiny from crews short of food or plunder. Seamen who were expert at navigation, like Black Bart, were soon promoted.

Medical items were also crucial to pirate survival. Blackbeard's last land siege was at Beaufort Inlet in Charleston, South Carolina. People said that after he took the town he demanded not gold but medical supplies.

Many pirates found fabulous wealth in gold, silver and precious stones. However, a pirate's plunder was more likely to be goods from merchant ships carrying silks, spices and other exotic goods from America, India and China back to Europe. This kind of cargo was of little use to pirates except as a source of ready cash. One pirate outfitted his ship with stolen silk sails to replace his own patched canvas ones. More often, captured cargo was sold on to dealers who could trade in ports without risking the gallows.

Landlubber lingo

Sailors and pirates have always used special nautical words, and some of them have been taken up by non-sailors as well.

Shiver me timbers! is an expression of surprise or annoyance (like 'Whoa!', 'Don't tell me!' and other less polite sayings). It first appeared in a book in 1834, and again in the famous pirate novel *Treasure Island* 50 years later. In olden times, 'shiver' meant 'break to pieces'. So 'shiver me timbers' to a pirate would mean 'May my boat break apart'. The saying became an oath, like 'I swear on my grave'. Shiver me timbers if I'm not telling you the truth!

To be **taken aback** means to be surprised at something.

If a ship's steersman was taken by surprise, the ship would naturally turn so that it faced into the wind. When this happened the sails were pressed back against the mast and the ship would be forced 'aback' – backwards.

Chock-a-block (or sometimes 'chockers' in Australia) means stuffed full.

Blocks (usually wooden) are part of a ship's 'block and tackle' – a system of ropes and pulleys used to hoist, lower and hold the sails of a ship. Chocks were pieces of wood placed between casks to prevent the casks from moving when the ship rolled. To be chock-a-block was to have so many blocks on the ropes that there wasn't room to fit a chock between them.

To give something a **wide berth** means to keep a good distance between you and it. A 'berth' is a place to moor a ship or boat.

Yo ho ho and a bottle of rum was commonly sung while sailors hauled ropes on their ships, and appears in the novel *Treasure Island*. The song starts:

Fifteen men on a dead man's chest,
Yo ho ho and a bottle of rum!
Drink and devil had done for the rest,
Yo ho ho and a bottle of rum!

4

BLACK-HEARTED SONS OF SEA DOGS

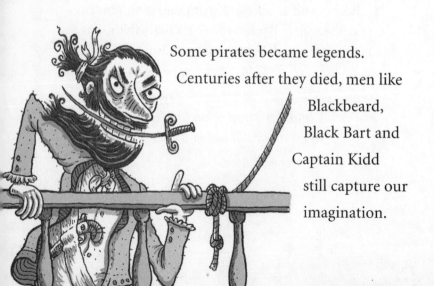

Some pirates became legends. Centuries after they died, men like Blackbeard, Black Bart and Captain Kidd still capture our imagination.

Blackbeard: blackest of the lot

Imagine it is the year 1720 and you are in a ship sailing quietly along the east coast of America. Suddenly, a ship bearing a black flag with a skeleton holding an hourglass appears on the horizon. A chase begins, and soon pirates are boarding your vessel. You see a large man with a thick black beard and ribbons twisted in his curls. His beard pours with smoke, his cutlass is clenched between his teeth and he's brandishing a pistol, with several more tucked into his sash. Look out, ye landlubbers, or Blackbeard will have your guts!

Blackbeard is probably piracy's most famous villain. His real name was Edward Teach, or Thatch. Like many pirates he started as a privateer, with a royal licence to plunder the ships of Britain's enemies.

Between 1716 and 1718 Blackbeard was a crew member with the pirate Benjamin Hornigold. Funnily enough, Hornigold had a reputation for politeness. Once he asked the crew of a plundered ship if they would mind giving up their hats, as he and his crew had drunkenly thrown theirs away. Blackbeard could also act the gentleman at times, and if a crew he was chasing surrendered he wouldn't harm them.

Hornigold left Blackbeard his ship, which Blackbeard renamed the *Queen Anne's Revenge*. He then began a life of pirating and plunder that became a legend.

Hands' sore knee and the sailor's sore hand

There were many rumours about Blackbeard. He was said to have shot his first mate Israel Hands under the table, shattering his knee and crippling him for life, simply to strike fear into the hearts of his crew and to make sure they obeyed him.

Another tale tells us that Blackbeard was once rejected by a young girl for another sailor. When Blackbeard later captured the sailor's ship, he recognised the girl's ring on the sailor's hand. He

cut off the hand, left the ring on and sent the grisly
package to the girl wrapped in a silver box.

Fire-breathing dragon

Once Blackbeard was said to have led his crew into his
hold, filled with smoke and burning brimstone.

'Come, let us make a Hell of our own,' he cried,
'and try how long we can bear it!'

He stayed there while the crew ran coughing out
into the fresh air, and cursed them all for cowards.

Blackbeard was so feared that many ships
surrendered at the sight of him. He built on his
fearsome reputation by lighting hemp coils dipped
into the flammable powder saltpetre and tied to his
beard. As he boarded a ship, his head smoked like a
fire-breathing dragon.

Although he captured at least 30 ships and attacked
the ports along the east coast of the Caribbean,
Blackbeard occasionally lived the life of an upstanding
citizen. Twice he received a pardon from the governor
of North Carolina, who was said to have shared in his

booty. He married Mary Ormond, a plantation owner's 16-year-old daughter, and built a house in North Carolina. He also had a base in the city of Nassau in the Bahamas.

Yo ho ho and a bottle...

Dead Man's Chest is a tiny island in the Caribbean Sea. According to legend, Blackbeard once marooned 15 sailors here with nothing but a bottle of rum and a cutlass each. When he returned he was surprised to find most of them still alive – drink and the devil had 'done for' the rest.

Blackbeard always returned to piracy, chasing naval and merchant ships alike. Eventually the people of North Carolina sent troops to rid the seas of this pirating menace.

Blackbeard's death was legendary. He died after reportedly receiving five musket wounds and more than 20 cuts in a sword fight against Lieutenant

Maynard. Maynard cut off Blackbeard's head and slung it from his bowsprit as proof that the dread pirate's life was over.

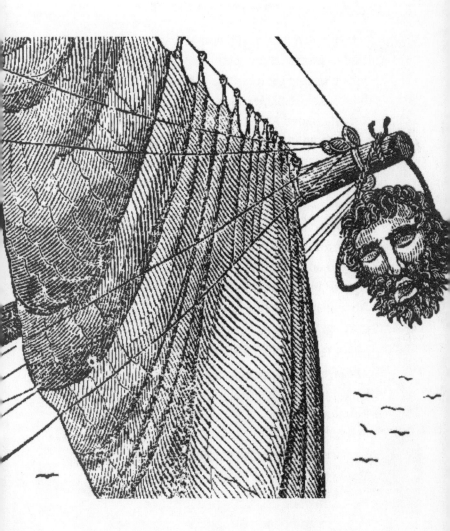

Yo ho ho and some fine new slaves

Pirates would take anything that was valuable – and that included people. Some pirates specialised in slave trading. Viking raiders captured many people and held them in thrall (as slaves). Merchant sailors such as Bartholomew Roberts traded African people bought or captured from their homes, sending them as workers to Caribbean settlements. In some countries, including Britain and France, slavery was legal until the late 1700s.

The Barbary corsairs were Moslem pirates from North Africa who raided ships from France, Spain, Italy and elsewhere. They sold the ships' crews at slave markets in Algeria, Morocco and neighbouring countries. Barbary pirates also kidnapped men, women and children from coastal villages in England and Ireland and took them back to Africa.

One of these captives was an eleven-year-old English boy called Thomas Pellow. He lived for 23 years in Morocco as a slave, house servant and soldier before escaping and sailing home. The white slave trade ended in 1816, when a British fleet attacked the city of Algiers and forced the ruler, the dey, to surrender. The commander of the fleet was Sir Edmund Pellew, grandson of Tom Pellow.

Black Bart

'A merry life and a short one shall be my motto.' So spoke Captain Bartholomew Roberts, also known as Black Bart. He was so successful that in just four years he captured more than 400 ships.

Roberts was born in Wales, but little else is known about his early life until he became the third mate of the slave ship *Princess of London*. In 1718 pirates captured some of the crew, including Roberts.

Roberts was an excellent navigator and despite being a prisoner soon became advisor to the pirate captain, Davis. After Davis was killed, Roberts was chosen to replace him.

Roberts was a strange man. He wore fine clothes and kept musicians aboard his ship, but tortured his prisoners. Roberts drank tea rather than alcohol and was deeply religious, but was feared for his cruelty.

He was very strict with his crew. They weren't allowed to gamble or have lights on after 8 p.m. (see pages 12–13), yet they never questioned his authority.

Here's an imagined extract from Black Bart's diary. (The bit about the ghostly 'shark' boat is completely made up!)

December 1718, journal of Captain Bartholomew Roberts
I was lookout on the Princess of London, *sailing along the West African coastline, and saw the pirate ship* Rapscallion *off the port bow. We made all possible sail, yet by noon the faster* Rapscallion *had caught up with us and its murderous crew boarded the* Princess *with few shots exchanged. Although the pirates were flying the dreaded red flag, they spared myself, the doctor and second mate Pip Moran. The poor wailing slaves, our cargo, they threw to the sharks. On account of this*

*barbarous act, I swore I would neither speak nor deal
with such a band of murderers. Captain Davis, with just
33 men aboard and short of a navigator, persuaded me
otherwise with the point of his pistol pressed against my
forehead. I could not stand against this man, near death
himself with starvation and desperate enough to commit
any crime.*

*I found the Captain surprisingly good company.
A religious man despite his trade, he held regular Sunday
services for his band of unruly thugs, and they were
devoted to him. The Captain's charts were not good, but
having sailed this coast for three years carting Negroes
to the British I was able to give the Captain useful
information. This allowed us to take three ships with very
little blood shed, and the Captain was so greatly pleased
that he offered to make me first mate. I agreed and was
soon entirely in his trust.*

*There was but one time the Captain and I found
ourselves in disagreement during our voyage together,
and that was when the Captain made an ill-conceived
plan to attack a town on the West African coast.
I doubted that the townsfolk would give in to our crew*

of only 35 men, but the good captain was set in his plan and sailed there straight away.

I was in the landing party that set out in the longboat that night and we heard from the town (where the Captain and the rest of the crew had landed) the sounds of baying hounds and angry yells. Three pirates escaped, and told how the Captain was struck down and his head most brutally severed by the neck. A loud wailing arose among the crew, and they bemoaned most heavily their ill-luck and their inability to bury the Captain in Christian fashion.

Seizing the moment, I persuaded them to follow me in a bold plan to retrieve both Davis's body and the treasure he had sought. I commanded the crew to cut down our sails and cover the longboat entirely in white canvas, so that it resembled a giant skeletal shark.

With this strange contraption we rowed each evening for a week into the bay, making the most ferocious sounds, and soon not a fishing boat would venture out upon the water. When at last we landed, half of the townsfolk fled in fear. Recognising the Governor of the town, whom I knew from my travels, I at once took him hostage. I persuaded him to give up a great quantity of silver and goods that we laboured mightily to cart back to the ship. Against their protests I took the Governor, his servants, bodyguard and musicians aboard the ship, of which I now became Captain. Then, using Davis's own effective means of persuasion, I enticed all but the Governor to join me. He I set down on a barren island 40 nautical miles off the coast, dressed only in his silk pyjamas.

Roberts sailed the West African coast, Canada and the Caribbean. He was finally killed in action after a battle with the pirate-hunting naval ship HMS *Swallow*. Shot in the throat, he was buried at sea as he had wanted before the *Swallow* overtook the pirates.

Who would you be?

**Surrender, ye blackguards!
I be the dread pirate . . .**

(insert name here)
_____

It's important to have a good pirate name. In the old days there was Blackbeard, and the Redbeards (the brothers Barbarossa). You could be the Dread Pirate So-and-So or the Wicked Such-and-Such. For instance, Bartholomew Roberts was known as both 'Black Bart' and 'the Great Pirate Roberts'.

In the days of the Barbary corsairs, Christian Europeans often changed their names once they converted to Islam. The Dutch privateer Jan Janz was one of these. He became Murad Rais, one of the most feared pirates and slave traders of the Mediterranean.

Want a quick pirate name? Begin with a good pirate colour, like red or black, or a nasty description, like dread or grim or terrible. Borrow an old-sounding surname, like Wills, Bonney or Morgan. Start writing your new name on all your school books – your teachers are sure to be terrified!

5

REBELS AND A PRINCESS

Piracy was a man's career. Women who were brave and desperate enough to become pirates also had to be really clever to get away with it.

One of them was Alwida, a Scandinavian princess who ran away to sea to escape marriage to Alf, the prince of Denmark. Legend says Alwida led an all-female crew and terrorised Baltic merchants so viciously that Prince Alf himself was sent to hunt her down. Alf captured Alwida and her crew, and she was so impressed with his bravery, she agreed to marry him after all.

Most pirates considered women to be bad luck, and wouldn't let them even come on board. Women who wanted to be pirates had to disguise themselves as men. In the cramped quarters of a pirate ship, this wasn't easy. But there were lots of dark corners to hide in while they undressed. As long as they could manage going to the toilet without being seen, in pirates' baggy clothes a woman could easily pass for a teenage boy.

Irish fire

Grace O'Malley, also known as Gráinne Mhaol, was an Irish pirate and rebel who attacked British shipping during the time of Queen Elizabeth I of

England. From her home on Clare Island, off the west coast of Ireland, she supported Irish nobles in their fight against invasion by Elizabeth's soldiers. Grace commanded 200 men and many ships inherited from her seafaring father.

Grace was well-born, the daughter of a chieftain, and married the heir to another chiefdom. She spoke Latin as well as Irish, and even gained an audience with Queen Elizabeth to ask for the release of her son after he was captured by the English.

Warrior widow

One of the toughest and most successful pirate leaders in history was a Chinese woman, Ching Shih. Shih inherited a huge fleet of sailing ships from her pirate husband Ching Yih after he died in a typhoon. Shih soon showed that she was more than Yih's match as a leader, with good business skills as well as a stomach for violence.

At the height of her powers Shih controlled a pirate army of more than 70 000, and many captains of her fleet were women. Shih had over 1800 ships at her command, split into the red, black, yellow and green fleets.

She kept careful records of all the plunder she took and distributed the loot according to her pirate code. This set of rules was so strict that pirates could face death for even landing on shore without permission. There were many violent raids carried out under Shih's name, and terrible punishments awaited prisoners, especially members of the Chinese army.

Five pirate heads hung on a wall, Honan, China

Shih eventually gave up piracy after some of her fleet betrayed her. She joined the army in trying to rid all pirates from the South China Sea. What happened to her later is unknown, but some believe that she turned her considerable business talents to smuggling.

Anne Bonny and Mary Read

Anne Bonny was a pirate active around 1720 who helped capture around 20 ships. Here's a version of her story written in diary form.

Anne Bonny

20 March 1720

Today is my birthday and I am sick of life on this island. It's no place for a County Cork woman, and my husband James is a fool. He's afraid I'll burn his sugar cane like I did my poor old dad's plantation, and so I might!

Last night to celebrate my coming of age I went to the Hovel 'n' Hole, the roughest pub in this God-forsaken island of New Providence. 'New Pigsty' more like.

5 April

I met that rascal pirate Jack Rackham last night. Jack's a real man, and James isn't a patch on him! He's taken a fancy to me with my dancing and my fine wit. We could be a real couple, and wouldn't the sparks fly then!

9 April

They've caught us! Who'd have believed that James and that Governor had it in them? They caught Jack and me red-handed, and threatened me with flogging unless I went back to James and the plantation, but I ain't never going back. Jack and I have other plans.

16 April

We've done it. Jack and I left that stinking pigsty and set sail in the Revenge with his crew – weren't they surprised! 'A woman on board is bad luck!', they said, but I stuck my papa's cane knife right into the belly of the old codger that spoke against me, and we'll not be hearing any *more complaints from him! We're for a pirating life and fortune, Jack and I, and no one's going to stop us!*

28 April

We've taken the sloop Charlotte's Fancy*. No gold on board, but a wealth of gear and rum – the crew was drunk for a week. They laughed till they cried when I donned the* Charlotte's *captain's gear and danced the decks till dawn! Poor old Jack tried to keep me in the cabin – says I'm a distraction to 'em – as if I couldn't take care of myself. My knife'll fix anyone tries to lay their hands on me! No, Jack can keep his cabin, for I've got my sights on other fish. Name's John Read and a finer man you never did see. Skin as smooth as a baby and a lovely head o' soft brown hair. That's what I like – a real gentleman pirate!*

5 May

You never did hear the like. I'd just got that fancy John in the hold for a bit of a private time, and what do I see?

A chest as soft as a mother's, and as womanly as any I'd ever seen! Mary Read's her real name – brought up John and started in life as a footboy! She was in love and married once, but Death carried off her man, so she took to the Navy and then pirating. Not to worry, her and me will have a life of fortune, I tell her, and death to any that tries to stop us – Jack included!

25 May

We've taken a trio of merchant vessels – Providence is the flagship and a fine little sailor she'll make. Jack's given me a brace o' pistols as a wedding present, seeing as he can't keep me from the action. Two men I killed, quick as any man and the rest of that jelly-livered lot had barely cocked their locks! Mary's with me, we'll show them what a fine Irish lass and a lovely London lady can get up to!

24 June

Mary's with child, she tells me. I'll have Jack's head if it's his, although she swears it's not. Still, feeling a bit poorly hasn't stopped her – five ships we've taken since last I wrote, and her in every action. I'll stand by her true, she'll have the little lad on ship if I have anything to say about it. Jack's taken badly after the last lot – no rum and the crew itching for some action. Of course, he blames the women on board! I'll show him a thing or two, he's no match for me or Mary if he tries anything with us!

17 August
Mary's showing now, and that cad Jack's got me in the same way. I'm sick as a yellow landlubber on his first sea trip and there's nothing but ship's biscuit to eat. No action since the Mary Ann went down to us and we left the crew marooned on a barren sandbar. There was not even a cask between them, poor devils, for we had to strip the ship of all, water, rum and even the rats, it's been that long since we took in food. The crew's near mad with hunger . . .

31 August

No doubt of it, I'm in the same boat as Mary. We'll be a fine pair of pirate mothers!

15 September

Finally struck a prize! Took the lovely Pearl *just out of Port Royal, loaded with pieces of eight and all manner of finery and frippery. We've dressed Mary up in women's gear for the first time, and didn't the crew look as flubbered as a drunken governor! Not a word from them, mind, I saw to that. Jack's been off the grog for once and sewed us up a new flag – black with a skull and two cutlasses crossed under. To put the fear in all who see us, he says, and Amen to that!*

6 October

That pirate chaser Captain Barnet's on our tail, and we're all quivering about what'll happen if he catches us. So far the wind is for us, but if it changes and sweeps back on us we're taken for sure. Jack's packed away the treasure and is holed up in the cabin, drunk as a pig, moaning how he's going to die on the gallows, the yellow dog.

9 October

We're had. Mary and I, on account of our condition, are being kept in the woman's prison in that rats' nest Port Royal, but the crew will hang for sure. Jack and the rest were so drunk that it was up to Mary and me to give Barnet's lot a bellyful of cutlass when they boarded.

Tomorrow I'll see Jack hang. Mary's looking bad and we're trying to trade what little we have to get her a decent cell where she may have the poor bairn she's carrying. They won't hang us at least . . . I'm not scared of anything, but God save me, I'm not looking to get my neck tied.

Anne Bonny escaped from prison with her life and vanished. According to some stories she later ran a pub, or married and started a new life. It is unlikely she continued as a pirate. Mary Read died in prison, either of fever or in childbirth.

According to Captain Charles Johnson's book *A General History of the Pyrates*, Anne Bonney's last words to Jack Rackham before he faced the gallows were, 'I am sorry to see you there, but if you had fought like a man, you need not be hanged like a dog.'

Sea-going superstitions

The idea that women were bad luck was one of many beliefs and superstitions shared by mariners.

The Kraken was a mythical monster of the deep. People said it looked like a giant cuttlefish and could suck ships to their doom. As it sank under water it created a whirlpool that sent ships to the seabed, much as a rubber duck is pulled towards the plughole in a bath.

Some people think that **mermaids** are a myth based on sightings of sea mammals called dugongs or manatees. Have you ever seen a dugong? If you have, you'll find it hard to imagine sailors could mistake one for a fair maiden with gold or green hair. In 1825 a 'mermaid from Japan' was one of the highlights of the famous Bartholomew's Fair in London. It turned out to be a woman with the skin of a large fish stitched to her skin to form a tail.

Sailors considered it **unlucky to set sail on a Friday**, particularly Friday the 13th, supposedly because Jesus was crucified on a Friday. Many ships would 'lie over' (stay anchored) until the next day to avoid this ill-luck. The first Monday in April was another unlucky day, as it was believed to be the birthday of Adam and

Eve's ill-fated son Cain and also the day on which he killed his brother Abel.

Whistling might anger St Anthony, patron saint of wind, and cause a storm to blow up.

Figureheads were carved wooden statues carried on ships as a mascot or good-luck token. They were originally strapped to the mast and may have been the carved likeness of ancient gods. Later they were moved to the front of ships, and took the form of lions, unicorns or dragons. Early figureheads were so ornate and heavy they made it hard for the ship to change direction. In the 1700s and 1800s the figureheads were much smaller and often featured the head and shoulders of the shipowner or a famous person. Naked ladies were also popular.

6

ROBBERS RIGHT ROYAL

Kings and queens sometimes asked fearless seamen to attack ships of the enemy. These government-sponsored seamen were called privateers.

Privateers carried letters of marque, documents from the king, queen or governor of their country saying the privateer was official and could not be prosecuted for piracy. In return, they gave part of the treasure they captured to their government. The rest they kept for themselves and their crew.

Fearless Francis's footprints

It was a stormy
night when English
privateer Francis
Drake and his men
attacked the town
of Nombre de
Dios in Panama.
They blew their
trumpets and
beat their drums,
carrying flaming
torches through
the city. The

townspeople awoke in terror, and poured into the
streets to ring the alarm bell and gather their weapons.
They rallied with the soldiers in the marketplace to
defend the great load of treasure the Spanish had stolen
from the native people of the New World.

The Spanish soldiers fired into the midst of Drake's
men, who shot back a volley of bullets and arrows.

When a group of Drake's men closed in on the east
side, the Spanish troops fled.

Drake led his men to the King's Treasure
House, where all the gold, pearls and jewels
were stored. It began to pour with rain.
Drake's men were afraid. The powder
for their guns was soaked and useless.
Drake had been shot in the leg during
the scuffle with the Spanish, and his
footprints filled with blood.

'We should go back,' Drake's crew cried.
'We can't fire our weapons and the Spanish
will kill us before we reach the ships.'

'You fools,' Drake replied. 'I've brought you to
the mouth of the treasure world. If you leave now,
you'll have no one to blame but yourselves!'

His men rallied behind him as Drake staggered to
the King's Treasure House. They battered down the
door and burst inside only to find . . .
nothing. The Treasure House was
empty. (Later they discovered that the
treasure ships had sailed six weeks before.)

Drake fainted from loss of blood (or from shock!) and had to be carried back to his ship.

An ordinary man would have sailed home defeated, but Drake stayed several months, waiting to attack a caravan of 170 mules heading for Nombre de Dios. This time he had better luck. Each mule was carrying 130 kilograms of silver, and in total there were 13½ tonnes of gold – enough to fill 80 medium-sized swimming pools. The total booty would be worth about $36 million today.

When Drake sailed back to England, he wasn't hanged as a pirate but hailed as a hero. Queen Elizabeth received him with honour. She loved to hear about his adventures and cheekily called him 'our pirate'. The gigantic pile of gold and silver Drake handed over to the Queen didn't hurt either.

Sir Henry Morgan, knight

Another gentleman pirate was Henry Morgan. Instead of dying a violent death at sea like most pirates, Morgan died a wealthy plantation owner, a knight and

the lieutenant-governor of Jamaica.

Henry Morgan had a letter of marque from the British government. His most famous raid was on the city of Panama, then a Spanish colony. He journeyed up the Cagres River with 1200 men in canoes. They marched through swamps for ten days. They soon ate all their provisions and were sick and starving. Some men were so hungry they ate the empty leather bags that had held their food.

Morgan's men were greeted outside Panama by 2500 Spanish foot soldiers, 400 soldiers on horseback, and 2000 wild bulls the Spanish hoped would trample Morgan's men to death. It didn't work out that way. By the end of the day, 600 Spanish soldiers were dead and the rest had fled. As the soldiers left, they lit barrels of gunpowder and blew up most of the buildings, leaving the beautiful city of Panama a smouldering ruin. Morgan and his men scoured the city, torturing anyone they could find to make them say where the treasure was. They found almost nothing.

Morgan had more success in other raids. In the West Indies, he captured millions of dollars worth of goods – equal to about $168 million today. He died when he was 53, wealthy but sick. Years of heavy drinking and partying had taken their toll.

Mystery man Jean Lafitte

One of the most mysterious privateers, Jean Lafitte appeared suddenly on the shores of New Orleans in 1803 and vanished just as quickly. Lafitte loved telling stories about himself and claimed to have fought with the Emperor Napoleon. He also described himself as a French nobleman whose parents were executed during the French Revolution. Historians suspect that he was actually born in Louisiana, USA.

He was a dashing and intelligent young man who could speak four languages and had an excellent knowledge of the marshy swamps of New Orleans. It was on the Bay of Barataria in New Orleans that Lafitte set up his kingdom of 1000 men. He had a fleet of 50 ships at his command, and they plundered Spanish shipments of silks, slaves and other goods, which the pirates took inland to sell. Like all privateers, Lafitte had a letter of marque. Lafitte's was from the Colombian government, which was fighting for independence from Spain.

Lafitte became a war hero when he fought against the British in the second War of Independence in 1812 and saved New Orleans. But eventually the American government turned against him. One morning they ordered Lafitte to leave his island or be 'blown to smithereens'. The next day Lafitte was gone. No one knows for certain what became of him, though legend says his ghost still walks through Louisiana, waiting to lead you to his buried treasure.

How strong is a storm?
How fast is a hurricane?

The **Beaufort wind scale** was invented in 1805 by Sir Francis Beaufort, an English admiral. Here are categories 7 to 12 – the wild ones!

No.	Wind speed	Description	Wave height	Effects on land and sea
7	28–33 knots *51–62 kms/hour*	Near gale	4 metres	• Sea heaps up, foams. • Trees bend, difficult for people to walk against wind.
8	34–40 knots *63–75 kms/hour*	Gale	5½ metres	• Waves breaking. • Twigs break off, cars veer on road.
9	41–47 knots *76–87 kms/hour*	Strong gale	7 metres	• Wave crests roll over. • Some damage to buildings etc.
10	48–55 knots *88–102 kms/hour*	Storm	9 metres	• Big waves, sea white, low visibility. • Trees uprooted.
11	56–63 knots *103–119 kms/hour*	Violent storm	11.5 metres	• Very big waves! • Widespread damage to buildings, roads, bridges.
12	64–80 knots *120+ kms/hour*	Hurricane	14+ metres	• Giant waves, air filled with foam and spray, sea totally white. • On land, even more damage.

Table adapted from Wikipedia

There is another wind scale for land, called the Newby wind scale. In a Newby **Strong gale**, children are blown over, and in Newby's **Whole gale**, adults are blown over.

Kidd's hidden treasure

Many movies and books have been made about William Kidd, privateer-turned-pirate – or was he? He certainly gained a fortune robbing ships in the Indian Ocean, but never thought of himself as a pirate, so he said.

Kidd ended up in prison and wrote to the British government begging for his life in return for a hidden stash of treasure. Perhaps his letter went something like this:

My name is William Kidd. I was born in Scotland in 1691, into a respectable family. Cursed misfortune has landed me in solitary confinement in this Stone prison, far from my wife and two daughters. If your honours my judges will listen, I will reveal the location of a treasure worth one million pounds sterling, in return for your honours' pardon for my supposed crimes.

Your honours will know I am well connected in the settlement of New York, where I have lived these five years as a merchant in tobacco and cotton.

In my youth, I was elected captain of a ship of privateers, the crew having decided to show the previous captain the error of his ways by pitching him overboard in his sleep. I sailed to the island of St Kitts and Nevis in the Caribbean, and out of respect for the King renamed my ship the Blessed William. *In service of His Majesty I then attacked such French shipping as was beneficial for the crown and myself, winning monies of great value.*

In truth I led a blameless life until misfortune befell me in December 1691. Then I was sent in the 34-gun, three-masted ship Adventure Galley with His Majesty's instructions to renew my efforts against the French, attack all pirates I encountered and take such prizes as were England's by rights.

Luck turned against me when my worthy and loyal crew were pressed into the service of His Majesty's Ship The Duchess and I was forced to hire thugs and brutes from the docks of New York. Intent on fulfilling my duty to the Crown, I in haste abandoned the ships I was escorting to carry out my orders of boarding likely prize ships. To my horror, the first ships I attacked had English captains. To pacify my crew I did share the treasures among them anyway, and with the utmost civility left these captains to sail home their empty ships.

During the following hideous journey to the African island of Madagascar, one-third of my crew died of cholera. Upon our reaching the island, many of the crew deserted and again I was forced to hire replacements .

It was then that traitor William Moore tried to incite my newly bought crew to mutiny. To quiet him I threw across the decks a bucket, which by chance broke open his skull, and did him grievous harm. He later died of the wound. The charge of murder and piracy for this action is greatly exaggerated, and I ask your honours to recall the circumstances in which this dreadful accident occurred.

Your honours, finally let me recall to you the great prize I took from the captain of The Quedagh Merchant, a vast ship of over 400 tons loaded to the brim with treasure and precious cargo. Knowing I was helping His Majesty I took the liberty of doling out £10 000 to the crew to ensure their loyalty, but secretly kept back vast quantities of gold, silver, silks and spices, which as mentioned I will reveal to you if you will consent to spare my life.

signed
Captain William Kidd

The English government
found treasure worth
£35 000 that Kidd buried
but not the full million he
had described, despite a
treasure hunt all over the
West Indies and also on
Gardiners Island off New
York. His story wasn't
believed and Kidd was
hanged for the crimes of
piracy and the murder of
William Moore. The rope
broke at the hangman's
first attempt. After the
second, Kidd's body was
trussed up and hung on
display for all to see.

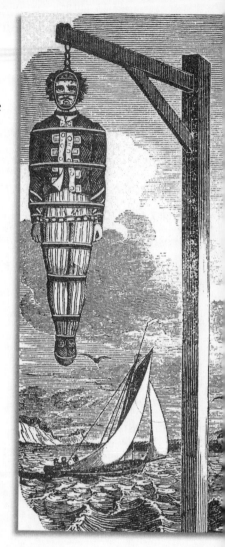

7

PIRATES' DOWNFALL

Pompey cleans up

There have been many attempts to clear the seas of
pirates, and some people did a pretty good job. The
Roman general Pompey the Great took on the pirates
of the Mediterranean more than 2000 years ago.
Even after Julius Caesar crucified his 300 pirates (see
chapter 1), there were still many more. The Romans
couldn't sail anywhere in peace!

With 124 000 troops and 270 ships, Pompey cleared
the Mediterranean of pirates in just three months.
Pirates were so terrified of him that when they saw his

ship they surrendered on the spot. At the end of three months he had captured and enslaved 846 pirate ships. Over 15 000 Mediterranean settlements and villages were so grateful that they agreed to be ruled by Rome, expanding the Roman empire nicely.

End of the 'Golden Age'

During the 1700s, pirates ruled the seas, from the Caribbean to the Indian Ocean. In 1720, there were around 2000 pirates in the Caribbean and North America. This may not sound like many, but at the time even a big city like New York had only 7000 people. So 2000 pirates was enough of a menace to make the ocean a dangerous place.

The downfall of the pirates came for many reasons. One was that governments stopped employing pirates and banded together against them. England, Spain and France had been warring against each other for years. Finally they decided that they hated pirates more than they hated each other. A treaty was signed in 1713. This meant both countries were able to tackle the pirate problem. England decided that instead of bringing captured pirates back to England, the governors of colonies could hang them on the spot. The bodies of the pirates were hanged in the ports as a fearsome reminder to all other pirates in the area about the fate that awaited them.

In 1856, most countries signed a declaration that made all letters of marque illegal. This meant no more privateers. Robbing another ship, no matter what country it was from, was piracy, and all pirates were to be hanged.

Outgunned

Once the English had finished their wars against France and Spain, they decided to use their navy to rid the seas of piracy. About 67 ships and 13 000 seamen were employed to seek out, capture and kill all pirates.

This was serious. The smallest navy ship was as big as the biggest pirate ship. Most navy ships had 70 guns, while pirate ships had only 10 to 20 guns. The pirates were outnumbered and outgunned, and often the only choice was surrender or fight to the death.

Before this time, only the captain of the pirate ship was hanged, along with a few others. But after 1716, every man or woman found guilty of pirating was to be sentenced to death. A reward was offered to anyone who captured or killed a pirate: £100 for a pirate captain ($4000 in today's money), £40 for a pirate officer and £20 for an ordinary seaman. Pirates were executed in lots of 10, 20, and even 50 at a time, and their bodies were left to rot along the shores.

Then there was a new decree. All pirates who surrendered before 5 September 1718 would receive a royal pardon. This, together with the reward, was an incentive for pirates to surrender, and then start hunting pirates who were still on the loose. Benjamin Hornigold was an ex-pirate who turned into a pirate-hunter. Hornigold made many captures before he perished after his ship struck a reef.

One by one, the big names were taken down. Blackbeard, Bartholemew Roberts and the brutal pirate Edward Low were all caught. In 1726, only six years after the pirate-hunting campaign began, there were fewer than 200 pirates and only six attacks.

The Golden Age of Piracy was over.

8

PIRACY TODAY

Pirates still exist today. In fact, there are hundreds of pirate ships around the world. The difference is that these men sail the seas in motorboats instead of tall sailing ships, and have guns instead of swords. There were 325 pirate attacks in 2004.

Being a pirate is still a profitable business. Modern pirates are after the money held in ships' safes, which can be up to tens of thousands of dollars. Pirates also steal cargo to sell onshore. Cargo ships and fishing vessels are warned to stay 300 kilometres away from the coast of 'pirate hotspots' like Somalia and Indonesia.

If you're thinking of embarking on a glamorous life of piracy, think again. It's a grim business. Pirates today are every bit as violent as Black Bart and other desperadoes of his time. They commonly kidnap people for ransom and may kill entire crews. The penalty for piracy in many countries is death – 13 pirates were executed in China several years ago, and many more are on 'Death Row'. At the very least you'd risk ending up in jail for a long time.

Are there pirates near YOU?

You can look up where pirates are most likely to attack on: www.icc-ccs.org/extra/display.php. Pirate hotspots are shown with coloured bubbles!

Digital pirates

Today all home movies come with a warning about piracy. This applies to anyone who copies DVDs or downloads videos, songs or other digital files without permission and without paying. Like piracy on the high seas, digital piracy is a crime (but not a hanging one!). It means the companies and artists who have been involved in making the movie or song don't get the royalties (income) they expect and deserve from the sale of CDs and DVDs.

Avast and ahoy there

There is one way to be a pirate without the hardships and the violence. Every year on 19 September it's Talk Like a Pirate Day. Talk Like a Pirate Day started with two people in 1995, and now millions of people all over the world take part by dressing up, playing pirate games and calling out 'Avast!', 'Ahoy' and 'Arrrgh!'. It's true!

Quiz

1 Which pirate set fire to his beard to make himself look more fearsome?

(a) Blackbeard ☐ (b) Bartholomew Roberts ☐
(c) Calico Jack ☐ (d) Francis Drake ☐

2 Pirates did not like women on board because they thought:

(a) women were too smart ☐ (b) women were bad luck ☐ (c) their dresses got in the way of the rigging ☐ (d) they always stole the treasure ☐

3 For dinner, pirates were most likely to eat:

(a) cake ☐ (b) turkey ☐ (c) emu ☐ (d) rats ☐

4 When pirates marooned someone, they

(a) dressed them in purple ☐ (b) covered them in coconut and honey ☐ (c) left them on a desert island to die ☐ (d) sang them a bedtime story ☐

5 What death awaited a pirate if he was caught?

(a) burning at the stake ☐ (b) hanging ☐
(c) shooting ☐ (d) being buried alive ☐

6 A red flag on a pirate ship meant:

(a) they thought you were a bull ☐ (b) red was their favourite colour ☐ (c) they would show no mercy ☐ (d) they were from China ☐

7 The Queen of England called the privateer Francis Drake:

(a) you black-hearted rogue ☐ (b) our pirate ☐ (c) our husband ☐ (d) our dog ☐

8 Most of the Spanish treasure came from:

(a) the English ☐ (b) pirate ships ☐ (c) the Incas ☐ (d) the bank ☐

9 Eating no fruit and vegetables gave pirates

(a) scurvy ☐ (b) the flu ☐ (c) measles ☐ (d) halitosis (bad breath) ☐

10 What did Julius Caesar do to the pirates who held him hostage?

(a) congratulated them ☐ (b) sank their ship ☐ (c) took them out for dinner ☐ (d) crucified them ☐

11 A landlubber is:

(a) a whale ☐ (b) a fat dog ☐ (c) someone who has no experience at sea ☐ (d) a rubber wetsuit ☐

12 What time did Black Bart's crew go to bed?

(a) 2 am ☐ (b) midnight ☐ (c) 8 p.m. ☐ (d) any time they liked ☐

ANSWERS: 1 a 2 b 3 d 4 c 5 b 6 c 7 b 8 c 9 a 10 d 11 c 12 c

HEATHER CATCHPOLE has been a pirate at birthday parties and has a husband who builds wooden boats in the garage. She frequently plans to sail to deserted islands. Heather is author of several children's books, including two other It's True! books, and works as a freelance science journalist.

VANESSA WOODS wanted to be a pirate until she found out that here were no toilets on board. Instead, she works with bonobos and chimpanzees in Africa. Besides two other It's True! books, Vanessa is also the author of the grown-up book about monkeys called *It's every monkey for themselves*.

 MIC LOOBY is a cartoonist for the *Herald Sun* newspaper and a columnist for *The Big Issue* magazine. This is the third It's True! book he has illustrated. His hobbies include chewing pens, humming softly and waiting for royalty cheques.

Thanks

To Alicia McKenzie, with thanks for her ideas and for my first fan letter, and to Aaron McKenzie, and Zara and Kalei Barger – I hope you enjoy it. Also to the buccaneers of the future, the good pirate Xander and the great princess Saskia.

Heather Catchpole

Thanks to Alice for her pirate books, Bronny, the dastardliest pirate of all, and Brian, my pirate in crime.

Vanessa Woods

The publishers would like to thank istockphoto.com and the following photographers for photographs used in the text: i pirate Joshua Blake, rodent Emilia Stasiak; viii ship Dane Wirtzfeld; 27 pistol Aleksandr Lobanov; 32 navigation equipment James Steidl; 73 treasure chest Sherwin McGehee; various scrolls Christine Balderas. Thanks also for the following: 19 illustrations by Georges Roux for the 1885 edition of *Treasure Island* by Robert Louis Stevenson; 22 map created by Robert Louis Stevenson; 41 Blackbeard's head, artist unknown; 52 Li Hung Chang's reminder to the lawless – five pirate heads hanging over the wall at Honan, China; 63 Sir Francis Drake, engraving by W. Hall; 67 Jean Lafitte, artist unknown; 70 US sloop of war *Kearsarge* 7 guns sinking the pirate *Alabama* 8 guns, off Cherbourg, France, published by Currier & Ives, New York, c. 1864; 73 Captain Kidd, from Charles Ellms, Pirates Own Book, 1837.

Thanks also to Ruth Grüner for alerting us to the white slave trade in Morocco.

Where to find out more

Websites

Pirates on Wikipedia

* http://en.wikipedia.org/wiki/
  Pirates

*Official site for Pirates of the
Caribbean*

* http://disney.go.com/
  disneypictures/pirates/

The Pirate's Realm

* www.thepiratesrealm.com

National Maritime Museum

* www.nmm.ac.uk/server/show/
  conWebDoc.159

Pirates on National Geographic

* www.nationalgeographic.com/
  pirates/

Pirates on the History Channel

* www.history.com/exhibits/
  pirates/

*Pirate lingo and Talk Like a Pirate
Day*

* www.io.com/~sj/PirateTalk.html
* www.talklikeapirate.com/
* www.seatalk.info/

Books

John Baur, Mark Summers, and
Dave Barry, *Pirattitude! So you
Wanna Be a Pirate? Here's How!*,
NAL Trade, 2005

Moira Butterfield, *Pirates &
Smugglers*, Houghton & Mifflin,
2005

Terry Deary & Martin Brown,
Pirates, (Horrible Histories
handbooks), Scholastic, 2006

John Farman, *The Short and
Bloody History of Pirates*, 21st
Century Books, 2002

John Matthews, *Pirates*, Atheneum,
2006

Richard Platt, *Pirate*, DK
Eyewitness Books, 2004

Philip Steele and David Cordingly,
World of Pirates, Southwater
Publishing, 2000

For teachers

David Cordingly, *Seafaring
Women: Adventures of Pirate
Queens, Female Stowaways,
and Sailors' Wives*, Random
House, 2007

Angus Konstam, *The History of
Pirates*, Mercury Books, 2005

*The Mammoth Book of Pirates:
Over 25 True Tales of Devilry
and Daring by the Most Infamous
Pirates of All Time*, Carroll
& Graf, 2006

Index